THE BIG BOOK OF
HORSES

HORSES

GROSSET & DUNLAP *Publishers* **NEW YORK**

Copyright, 1951, by Grosset & Dunlap, Inc. Lithographed in the United States of America
ISBN: 0-448-02241-9 (Trade Edition)
ISBN: 0-448-03692-4 (Library Edition)

1974 Printing

THE ARABIAN • The Arabian stallion is the very height of quality in horse breeds. He is the most valuable of foundation stock, and alone possesses the quality, soundness, stamina and vitality to improve every other breed.

The Arabian is different in several ways from all other horses. For example, the common horse has nineteen pairs of ribs, and the Thoroughbred eighteen. The Arabian has only seventeen or sometimes eighteen pairs of ribs. This gives him greater weight-carrying power and greater muscle strength. The texture of the Arabian's bone is like ivory, denser and stronger than the bone of the ordinary horse. His ribs are "well sprung," which means they arch outward. This gives more lung space and accounts for his great endurance.

Compared with the common horse, the Arabian's eyes are larger and much lower in the skull. This is important because it allows more space for the brain, which accounts for his greater intelligence. His forehead is extremely broad, his jaw deep and wide, with a fine, small muzzle. His nostrils are large and flexible, his ears small and sharp, his neck arched, his skin a dark gray. Generally the Arabian stands about 14:3 to 15:1 hands high. (A horse's height is measured in "hands," each equal to 4 inches, from his withers to the ground. 14:3 means 14 hands plus 3 inches, or a total of 59 inches.)

1. A foal fifteen minutes old.

4. A young Arabian colt feeling frisky.

2. The foal half an hour old, and trying to stand on his own four feet.

5. Mare and three-months-old foal.

3. The foal's first meal, about an hour after birth.

6. Palomino mare and colt.

7. A very strong Belgian draft-horse colt.

COLTS AND THEIR TRAINING

At well-run ranches and farms, new baby colts, or foals, as they are called, start their education a day or two after they are born. A soft rope halter is put on the foal and he is led gently around. When he responds, he is given a bit of sweet feed. When he is three months old, he is taken away from his mother and fed oats. By now, he is "gentled," and has learned the feel of hands. During his first winter and summer he lives outdoors in the pasture. The following fall, he is roped and gently retaught his early training. The trainer also puts a bridle with a light snaffle bit on him, and he is led by reins. A blanket is put on his back, so that he will get used to the feel, and not be frightened when his first saddle is placed on his back. The girth of the saddle is gradually drawn tighter. Then his first rider mounts, and again he is led about. Next he is allowed to walk, unled, around the training pen with his rider pulling his reins quite firmly. After this he is again let free to run and play with the other yearlings until he is about thirty months old. Then his education is resumed. Now he learns to stop and start, to trot with rider up, and to break into a canter from a walk. He has graduated from grammar school and is ready for his special training.

8. The colt tastes grass for the first time. He can reach it only by bending his long forelegs.

9. Two pals. Young colt with his big boy friend.

10. The colt of a gaited horse. Notice that his stride has style from the start.

THE POLO PONY • The polo pony is a very special horse, with special qualities and special training. He must be able to stop and turn in a flash, to break into a dead run at the slightest sign from his rider, and have enough courage to run amidst swinging mallets and other horses bearing down on him. Experts say that in relative importance, the horse contributes seventy-five per cent or more to the game, and the rider twenty-five per cent or less. No wonder it takes three to five years of constant schooling to train the polo pony.

HORSE RACING and the JOCKEY • Speed, stamina, excitement, thrills, danger, courage —these are all part of horse racing. Both the jockey and his Thoroughbred racer must have courage to be champions. It requires courage to urge a horse into openings at exactly the right moment while at a dead run. The jockey must be a great rider, to know just how much endurance his horse has in reserve for the end of the race, what speed his horse can command, and just when he can command it. Race horses are all Thoroughbreds, and are given special training.

CIRCUS HORSES • The beautiful white horses used by the acrobats who ride bareback are one of the familiar sights we love to see at the circus. These are highly trained horses of draft-horse breeds, and they can do wonderful stunts. They are chosen for smartness of gait at a slow, even canter, for broadness of back to give the acrobat a platform on which to stand or sit, and for flatness from hip to hip across the croup.

A special type of circus horse is the "High School Horse," who is a solo performer. He gives various performances, and he cakewalks or tangos to music. Often he has a lady as his rider.

Still another circus horse is the "Liberty Horse." This horse works in a group with other horses, performing acts without a rider, at the direction of the ringmaster.

1. Portrait of a Shetland pony.

2. A young boy jumping his pony (bigger than a Shetland) in a horse show.

Here are the picturesque names of the other main English pony breeds, and the maximum heights they can be registered as pure:

Connemara	14:2 hands
Dales	14:2 hands
Dartmoor	12:2 hands
Exmoor	12:2 hands
Fell	14 hands
Highland	14:2 hands
New Forest	12-14 hands
Welsh	12 hands

3. A little girl on her crossbred Western pony.

4. A group of Shetland ponies on a farm in the Shetland Islands.

PONIES • The Shetland is the purest and smallest of the pony breeds. He makes a wonderful pet, and is quiet, trustworthy, sure-footed, intelligent and good-natured. The Shetland comes from the rugged Shetland Islands north of Scotland, and is one of the very oldest breeds of ponies. Until he is two years old, his coat is wool rather than hair. At four years old, he is capable of carrying a man's weight. He lives often as long as thirty years. In the early days in England, he was used to haul coal in the mines. Today, besides being a pet, he makes a fine show pony, and is ridden in jumping classes too. Usually he takes jumps of two feet up to two and one-half in the show ring. A purebred Shetland is never more than 10:2 hands high, or 42 inches. The smallest mature Shetland on record was only 6:2 hands high, or 26 inches.

5. Two children on their ponies at the start of a hunt. Welsh ponies are often used in hunting. Any properly trained pony that is large enough, and can jump, can be used to hunt.

DON'TS IN HORSEMANSHIP

1. Don't let your horse start until you are completely in the saddle. Then give him the signal.
2. Don't rush to the front and constantly try to be the leader when riding with other riders.
3. Don't feed your horse while his tack (bridle, saddle, martingale) is being put on, or while he is being groomed.
4. Don't let your horse stop to eat grass, or reach out for leaves on a ride.
5. Don't gallop your horse for too long a time.
6. Don't ride on hard roads if it can be avoided; keep to the soft shoulder. Never cross or turn on hard-surfaced roads, because horses' shoes slip easily on these surfaces.
7. Don't be just a passenger on your horse.
8. Don't fall in love with your horse, because if you do, you'll never want to sell or exchange him for a better one.

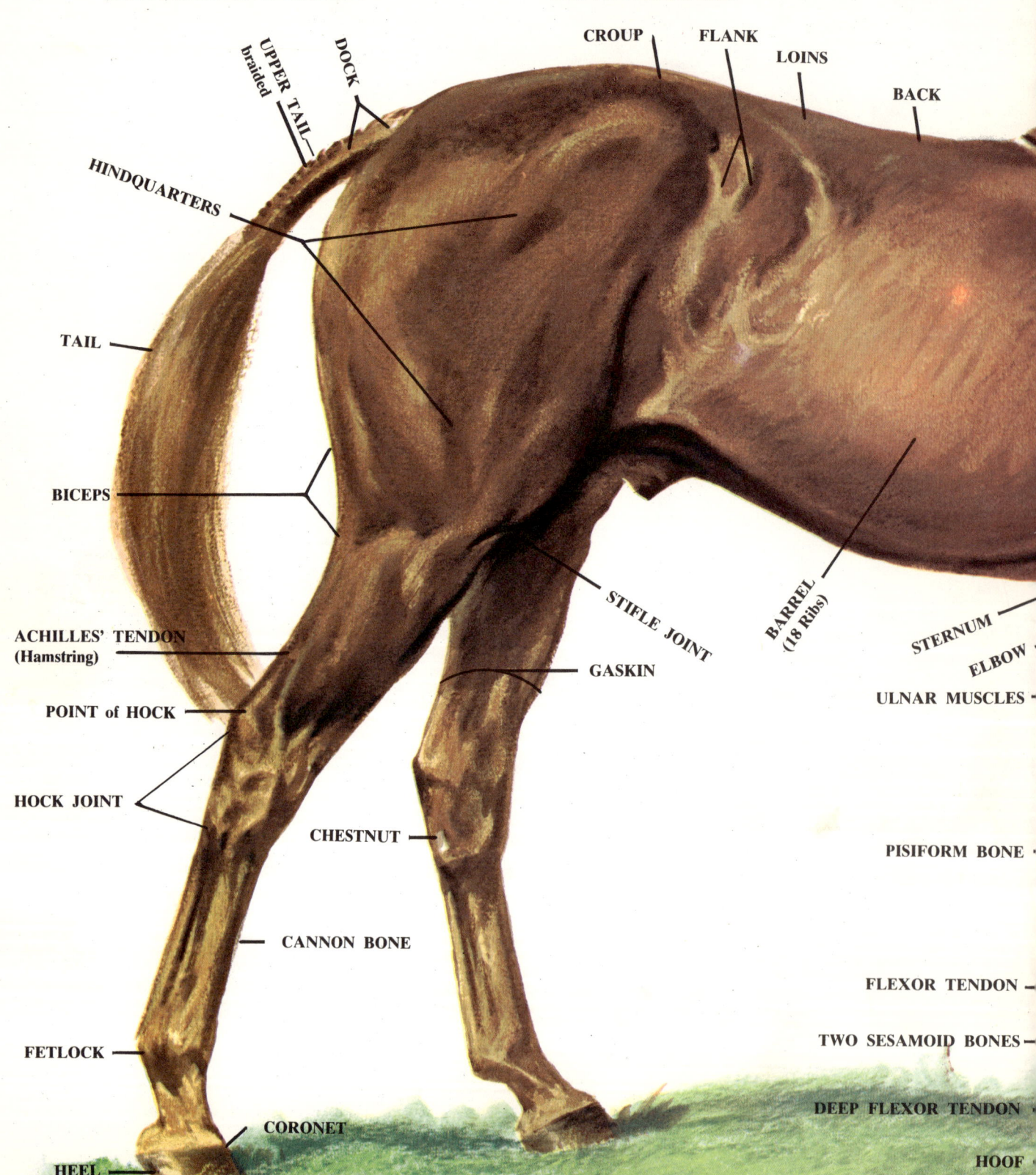

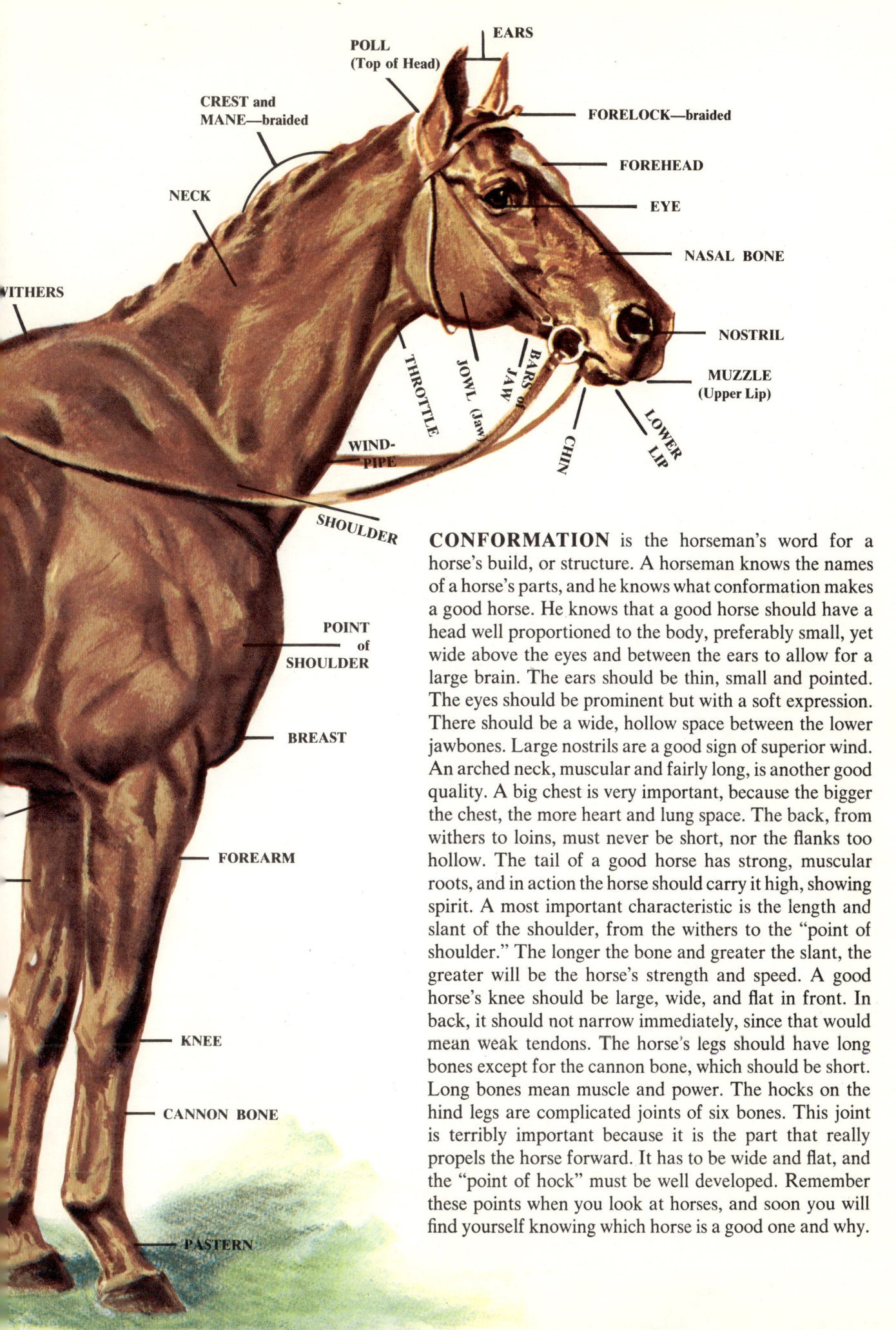

CONFORMATION is the horseman's word for a horse's build, or structure. A horseman knows the names of a horse's parts, and he knows what conformation makes a good horse. He knows that a good horse should have a head well proportioned to the body, preferably small, yet wide above the eyes and between the ears to allow for a large brain. The ears should be thin, small and pointed. The eyes should be prominent but with a soft expression. There should be a wide, hollow space between the lower jawbones. Large nostrils are a good sign of superior wind. An arched neck, muscular and fairly long, is another good quality. A big chest is very important, because the bigger the chest, the more heart and lung space. The back, from withers to loins, must never be short, nor the flanks too hollow. The tail of a good horse has strong, muscular roots, and in action the horse should carry it high, showing spirit. A most important characteristic is the length and slant of the shoulder, from the withers to the "point of shoulder." The longer the bone and greater the slant, the greater will be the horse's strength and speed. A good horse's knee should be large, wide, and flat in front. In back, it should not narrow immediately, since that would mean weak tendons. The horse's legs should have long bones except for the cannon bone, which should be short. Long bones mean muscle and power. The hocks on the hind legs are complicated joints of six bones. This joint is terribly important because it is the part that really propels the horse forward. It has to be wide and flat, and the "point of hock" must be well developed. Remember these points when you look at horses, and soon you will find yourself knowing which horse is a good one and why.

CUTTING PONY and the QUARTER HORSE • The cowboy and his fast, strong and agile cutting pony can separate the beef steers from the herd or, as shown here, keep the cattle together in the herd. The cutting pony is highly trained, and will follow whatever steer the cowboy spots, and quickly drive it through the main herd to the holding herd. The best cutting ponies are descended from the earliest type of American-bred horse, called the Quarter horse. The

first Quarter horses were developed by the earliest settlers in Virginia, over two hundred years ago. They were called Quarter horses because they raced on short, quarter-mile paths, since there were no real race tracks in those days. Later they were crossbred with Thoroughbreds, which improved their quality and performance. Special breeding for fast, short dashes makes the Quarter horse an ideal cow horse. This has been his main function in modern times.

1. The show horse's very stylish trot, head and tail up, feet lifted smartly, all with precision.

2. The walk of the flat racer, showing the seat and hands of the jockey.

3. The slow, relaxed canter of the show horse in the ring.

4. A racing trotter, in a fast trot.

HORSEMANSHIP

Good horsemanship should be the aim of anyone who loves horses and loves to ride. Let us take an imaginary ride to explain the points of good horsemanship. When you are properly dressed and ready to go, approach your horse's head from the left side and quietly see to it that the bit or curb chain is not too tight. Pat his neck, slowly sliding your hand to the saddle's girth to see that it is neither too loose nor too tight. Before you put your left foot in the stirrup, pick up your reins gently in your left hand, to be sure that they are just long enough to give you control of the horse's head. Then, with reins in hand, grasp a lock of his mane. Face toward the back of the horse, take hold of the stirrup strap just above the stirrup with your right hand, put your left foot into the stirrup and then, with your right hand on the pommel of the saddle, quietly lift yourself into the saddle. Be sure not to touch the horse with your right leg as you swing it over his back.

Once you are in the saddle, adjust the reins so that they bring the bit in slight contact with the corners of the horse's mouth. Keep your hands down and about four inches apart. Keep your hands and your feet still, since any moves indicate a message to the horse. Have the horse stand quietly a moment before giving him the signal to move off.

For the first few minutes, walk your horse to limber him up and become acquainted with his mouth and action. Then try a slow trot for five minutes.

Remember that if he is trained at all, the horse interprets moves as signals with a meaning. Be careful to avoid confusing him during the start of the ride. Avoid unnecessary moves such as jerking the reins, kicking him in the side, or fussing with the stirrups.

Keep your knees in, your heels down and your toes pointing straight ahead with the balls of your feet pressing on the stirrups. You'll find that if your feet are pointed right, it will help hold your knees and

5. This is the gait of the pacer, who supports himself alternately on the legs of one side and then the other. Note the difference from the trotter.

6. This gait is the single-foot rack, illustrated by a show horse. In this gait, each of the horse's feet strikes the ground singly, and there are alternately one and two feet on the ground.

7. This is the walk of the hunter. Note the proper seat and hands of the rider.

inner calves firmly against the horse's side. Sit toward the front of your saddle.

Your seat will be a good seat if your weight is in balance and in rhythm with the horse. Your seat will change depending on the particular performance of the horse. The balancing center of the horse is between his front feet and his withers. Therefore, a racing jockey, who must strive for great running speed, puts his knees as nearly as possible on this center of balance. Your knees and calves will determine your seat. Stirrup straps, of course, must be adjusted in length accordingly.

The steeplechase jockey's seat is less forward than the racing jockey's, with longer stirrups, because he must be secure enough to handle the jumps and be able to shift his weight in coordination with the horse's jumping.

The hunting seat is forward in the saddle, with longer stirrups, because the pace is slower and care must be taken to avoid falls.

The Western seat and saddle are for riding long hours over rough country. The rider sits down into a deeper saddle, where he will interfere least with the constant change in action.

Your hands, which means the handling of the reins, are very important to good horsemanship. Good hands have a natural, sensitive touch, developed through experience and common sense. They must be sensitive to the horse's reaction, light, yet positive. They should be flexible and alert, never heavy or severe. Good hands make few moves, but these always give clear directions to the horse. Lightness and balance in the touch of the rider's hands can actually make the movements of the horse lighter and more balanced. Bad hands can ruin even a good horse's disposition and spoil his training in a short time.

8. A racer in full gallop or run.

THE THOROUGHBRED HUNTER

Fox hunting on horseback is one of America's very oldest sports. The champion Thoroughbred hunter is one of the most magnificent types of horse. He must have speed, strength, and endurance enough to run by the hour across the countryside. He should also be comfortable to ride and easy to control. If he is "truly made," or of sound conformation, 16:3 hands is big enough for a good hunter. Look for these characteristics in a hunter: a long, sloping shoulder for strength; a "deepness in the heart," which means a big distance from the withers to the bottom of the chest in back of the elbow; a big "front" or chest for wind; a long but powerful neck from withers to poll; a rather short back from the withers to the croup; deep, sloping hindquarters with lots of muscle into the gaskin; strong forearm muscles; hard, tense tendons behind the cannon bone; and a long pastern sloping at an angle to the ground.

HACKAMORE

RACING BIT

BOY'S WESTERN SADDLE

DOUBLE BRIDLE
CURB AND SNAFFLE BIT
WITH RUNNING MARTINGALE

BITS • The bit is the metal part of the bridle that is inserted in the mouth of the horse. The bit is very important in horsemanship because it is the main instrument whereby the rider communicates his wishes to the horse. There are dozens of different kinds of bits, some gentle and some severe. All are variations of two main types, the snaffle bit and the curb bit. These, plus the Pelham bit, which is a combination of the two, are the ones chiefly used. The snaffle bit exerts pressure on the corners of the lips of the horse's mouth. There are two types of snaffle bits; the plain or unjointed snaffle, and the broken or jointed snaffle. The broken snaffle pinches the horse's mouth when it is pulled and can be quite painful. It should be adjusted so that it just barely touches the corners of the lips. The curb bit is made so that by pulling on the reins, the rider exerts pressure on the jaw with the chain shown above, as well as upon the bar in the horse's mouth. It can be a very severe bit. Adjust the curb chain so loosely that you can easily put two fingers between the chain and the groove of the horse's chin. The Pelham bit is a combination of the curb and the snaffle, but with just one bar in the horse's mouth. With the double bridle, two bars go into the horse's mouth,

RACING SADDLE

PELHAM BIT

SNAFFLE BIT AND STANDING MARTINGALE WITH ENGLISH SADDLE

both the snaffle-bit bar and, about an inch lower, the curb bit. The hackamore is a kind of bridle without a bit. The horse learns to respond to the pressure of the hackamore's band across his nose and against his sensitive chin and jawbones. The martingale is a device by which the rider controls his horse's head. The standing martingale is connected to the noseband of the bridle, the neck strap and the girth of the saddle. It prevents the horse from throwing his head too high. The running martingale directs the pull of the reins so that it brings the bit down against the bottom of the horse's jaw. It makes the horse bend the upper part of his neck.

SADDLES • Remember that the good horseman never has a larger or heavier saddle than necessary. The worst riders pile on heavy Western saddles because they want to look like cowboys and because they want to feel secure. The English saddle is designed for general riding pleasure and efficiency. This is the saddle you should use when you are learning to ride. The racing saddle is a special saddle weighing only 1½ to 3 pounds.

DRAFT HORSES • The big work horses popular in America are usually Percherons, Clydesdales, Suffolks and Belgians. These breeds produce horses weighing from 1500 to over 2000 pounds. Usually they are from 16 to 17:2 hands high, although their height is not as important as their compactness and muscle. The smaller work horse used for general light farm work is a crossbreed, stemming from any one of the recognized draft breeds bred with a mare of mixed breed. He is called a "farm chunk." A good draft horse must have a large foot. "No foot, no horse," is the saying. He needs a long, slanting pastern and a concave sole. He should move his feet

and limbs straight ahead, picking his feet up with a snap to show the sole of the hoof as he steps. He should have a powerful neck and should carry his head high when he is not working. His shoulder should not slant as much as other breeds, and must be smooth so that the collar fits well to avoid soreness. You will see that he has a massive chest, broad and deep, that his loins are closely and heavily muscled, and that his hocks look deep from the side, and are smooth and well defined. Perhaps some day the work horse will give way to the machine, but it will take a long time for the machine to build up a comparable record of labor.

THE POLICE HORSE • This police horse, like most police horses, is of the Morgan breed or family. He is named a Morgan horse after Justin Morgan, the very first horse in his line, a little bay stallion weighing only 950 pounds, foaled back in 1793. No one knows his exact breeding, but the Morgan breed has since done everything from general farm work to catching criminals. He is truly an American breed and the only one that derives from an individual horse. Today he has been developed into a much larger horse of from 15 to 16:2 hands, weighing 1,000 to

1,150 pounds. He is strong, intelligent, of a friendly disposition and known for his great courage. The best police forces use him, and specify that he must be between four and seven years old, weigh between 1,000 and 1,150 pounds, and stand 15:3 to 16:1 hands high. He must be a bay or a rich mahogany brown in color, with long mane and tail. Neither a whip nor a sharp word is used in his training. He is taught to back, step sideways, stand perfectly still, rear and plunge on command. He is a great sprinter and a bull for endurance.